The Amazing
Human Body

Rob Waring, *Series Editor*

NATIONAL
GEOGRAPHIC
LEARNING

Australia · Brazil · Mexico · Singapore · United Kingdom · United States

Words to Know

This story is about the almost seven billion human bodies that live on our Earth today.

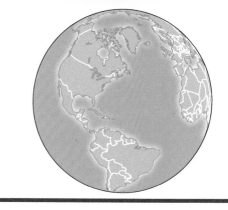

A **The Human Body.** Read the paragraph. Then match each word with the correct definition.

The smallest part of the human body is the cell. Cells compose every single part of the body. The average human adult body comprises close to 100 trillion cells. There are certain cells that come together to make muscles, which help us move. Other cells work together as tissues to perform certain functions as organs. These cells are usually part of specific systems designed to perform essential life functions, such as the lungs, which allow us to breathe.

1. cell _____

2. trillion _____

3. muscle _____

4. tissue _____

5. organ _____

6. lungs _____

a. a type of body part that performs a specific function, such as the heart

b. two breathing organs in the chest that supply oxygen (O_2) to the blood

c. the basic unit of all living things

d. a thousand billion (1,000,000,000,000)

e. body parts that connect to bones and make the body move

f. a group of connected, similar cells that perform a certain function together or form part of an animal or plant

B **Organ Systems of the Body.** Read the definitions. Then write the letter of the correct system next to each description.

1. _____ The circulatory system is related to the pumping of blood through the body by the heart.

2. _____ The digestive system transforms food into energy and rids the body of waste.

3. _____ The nervous system transmits informational signals from the brain through the body.

4. _____ The reproductive system is related to the production of babies.

5. _____ The respiratory system is related to the process of breathing.

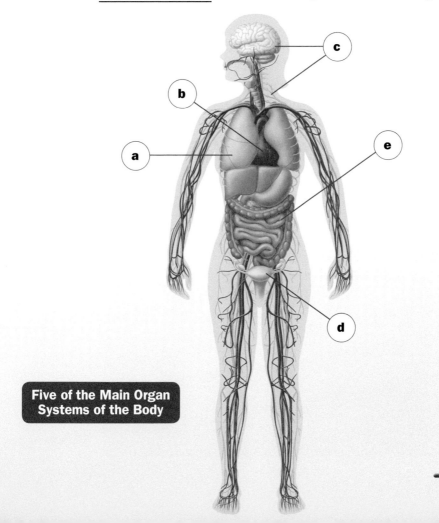

Five of the Main Organ Systems of the Body

The human body is a truly amazing 'machine.' In fact, no machine made by humans can match the impressive actions the human body performs every day. Walking around the house, shopping, or simply breathing may seem like easy activities. But what about when we exercise? What happens when we run, swim, surf, ski, work out, or dance? No other animal on Earth can perform such a wide variety of activities. That's when the remarkable human body really shows how wonderful its range of action really is.

The story of our body is one of incredible statistics, and when one takes a closer look at them, the numbers are quite astonishing. Our lungs, for example, have the capacity to take in 66 liters* of air each minute when we exercise. Our hearts pump more than 7,570 liters of blood each day, and it takes more than 600 muscles to keep us moving in every direction. The body is able to move forwards, backwards, upwards, downwards, and even spin in circles. There's absolutely no doubt that the human body is one of the most amazing natural instruments in the world.

---

*See page 24 for a metric conversion chart.

CD 1, Track 03

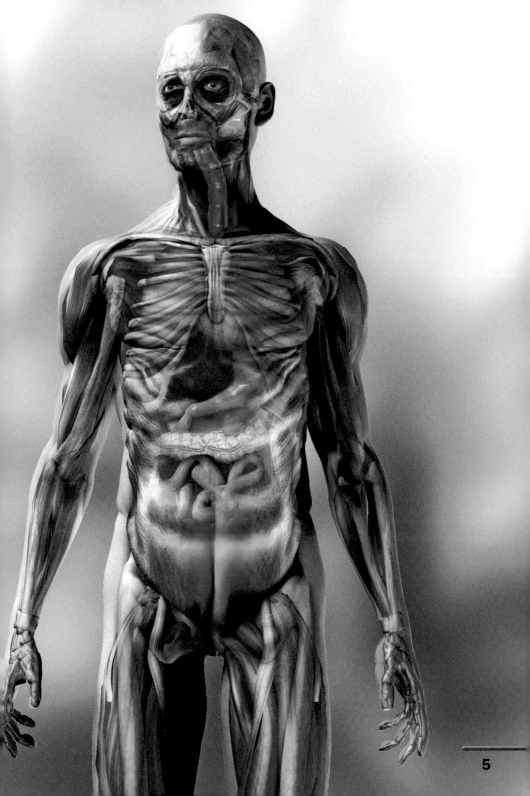

How does the body actually work? Of what is it composed? Naturally, such a complex machine contains several levels of structure. Cells are the smallest level of the body's organization, and—like all other living things—human beings are made up of large numbers of cells. In the case of humans, there are over 100 trillion of them in the average-sized body.

At the next level of organization, individual cells are arranged into tissues, a collection of similar cells that are grouped together to perform a specialized function. The heart, for example, is made up of heart muscle tissue. There are four primary tissue types in the human body: **epithelial**[1] tissue, connective tissue, muscle tissue, and nerve tissue.

At the more advanced level, different kinds of tissue come together to form organs, such as the heart, the lungs, and the stomach. There are numerous organs that exist within the body, but in order to be effective and efficient they must be organized into systems. Several organs working together create an organ system. There are ten major organ systems in the human body, including the circulatory system, the respiratory system, the digestive system, the nervous system, and the reproductive system. Each of these organ systems performs a special job within the body.

_____

[1] **epithelial:** of or relating to the layer of cells that covers all the open surfaces in the body, such as the skin

A human cell viewed through a microscope appears very complex.

Predict

Answer the questions. Then scan page 9 to check your answers.

1. How many times a minute does the average heart beat? a) 33 b) 72 c) 90

2. How many minutes does it take for the blood to circulate around the body?
   a) less than one b) more than two c) about four

3. How many kilometers of air passages are there in the human body?
   a) almost 50 b) about 360 c) more than 2,400

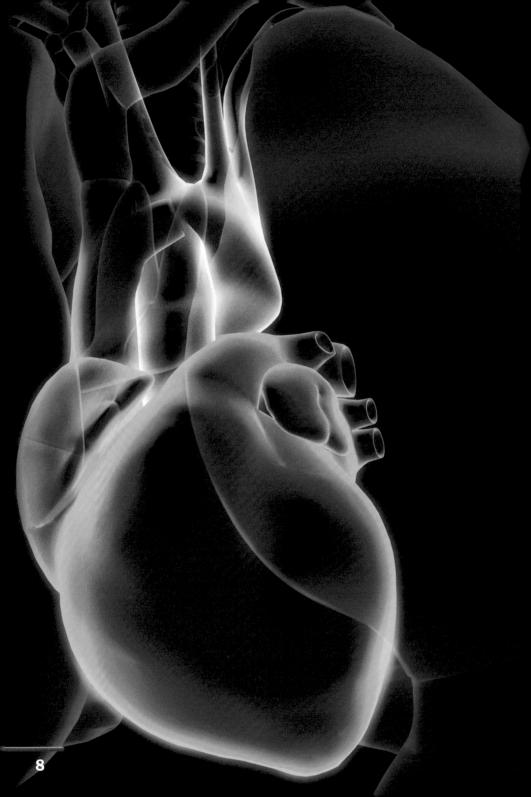

The circulatory and respiratory systems supply energy to the body 24 hours a day, every day of one's life. The major organs of these systems are the heart and the lungs. Together, the two coordinate to create what could be considered to be the engine of this fantastic machine.

The heart is the major organ of the circulatory system, and the 'pumping center' of the body. Although quite small in comparison to the proportions of the rest of the body, this powerful little organ works incredibly hard and completely automatically. No other muscle is as strong as the heart, making it one of the principal organs in the entire human body. The heart is really nothing more than a pump, composed of millions of muscle cells, that pushes blood throughout the body. It beats approximately 72 times per minute, or 100,000 times a day, or 36 million times a year—every day of our lives. The heart pumps the blood on a complete trip around the body in less than a minute, transporting all of the materials that help our bodies function and removing the waste products that we don't need.

The most important organs of the respiratory, or breathing, system are the lungs. The two lungs are located in the chest of the body on either side of the heart. Day after day they expand and contract, pulling in oxygen from the air and delivering it to the body through more than 2,400 kilometers of air passages. The principal function of these valuable organs is to transport oxygen from the atmosphere into the **bloodstream**,[2] and to transmit unwanted gases that have accumulated in the bloodstream out of the body.

---

[2]**bloodstream:** the flow of blood through the body

The body and all of its organ systems get their energy from food. Turning the meals we eat into the energy used by our bodies is the job of the digestive system. When we eat foods—such as bread, rice, meat, and vegetables or other forms of **nourishment**[3]—they're not in a form that the body can use. Food and drink must be converted into smaller **molecules**[4] before they can be absorbed into the blood and carried to cells throughout the body. Digestion is the process by which food and drink are broken down into their smallest parts, or **nutrients**,[5] so the body can use them to build and nourish the cells and provide energy for their activities.

_____

[3]**nourishment:** the health components needed by the body for energy in the form of food
[4]**molecule:** the smallest unit of the elements in a substance
[5]**nutrient:** any of the substances contained in food that are essential to life, such as protein, vitamins, and minerals

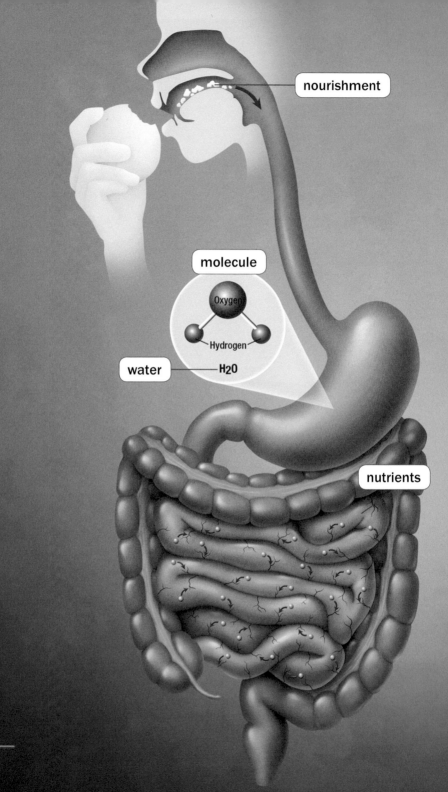

nourishment

molecule

Oxygen

Hydrogen

water — H2O

nutrients

Digestion involves mixing food with digestive juices, moving it through the digestive system, and breaking it down into smaller more easily absorbed molecules. Digestion begins in the mouth, when you eat and **swallow**,[6] and is completed in the small intestine. First, the act of swallowing sends food down the esophagus, or throat, into the stomach. Then, like a food mixer, the stomach contracts to break this nourishment down, helped by **acid**[7] and **enzymes**.[8] These nutrients, which are now liquid, then travel into the small intestine, which can be over six meters long. It is here that most nutrients are transferred into the bloodstream. Waste products from the entire process are then sent out of the body through the large intestine. It's an aggregate process involving several different parts, which makes it an astonishingly efficient and truly amazing system.

---

[6]**swallow:** take food or drink into the throat from the mouth
[7]**acid:** a substance or liquid that can chemically react with, and sometimes break apart, other materials
[8]**enzyme:** a natural chemical in living cells that helps make them work

In contrast to the digestive system, the brain functions at a higher level. It's the nerve center of the body, and it controls the entire 'system of systems.' Although it's the source of all thought and action within the body, the human brain doesn't look at all like a super-computer. With its lined surface and strange shape, it looks more like a strange fruit that has gone bad. It too, like the heart, is relatively small in proportion to the rest of the body—about the size of a grapefruit—but it's the most complex object on Earth.

The brain not only affects and governs everything we do, and how we think, feel, and act, but it also affects what kind of individuals we are. In fact, it controls the entire nervous system of the body and regulates virtually all human activity. Automatic, or 'lower,' actions, such as heart rate, respiration, and digestion, are unconsciously governed by the brain. In other words, they just happen without us having to think about them or tell them to happen. Complex, or 'higher,' mental activities, such as thought and reason, are consciously controlled within the brain, which means that these are directed by mental processes and intent.

The brain contains up to 100 billion nerve cells. The nerve cells' job is to transmit signals through the brain at over 320 kilometers an hour. The brain, **spinal cord**,[9] and nerves make up the central nervous system—and all work together to control the body's activities. Despite the way it looks, the brain actually functions at the level of a super-computer.

---

[9]**spinal cord:** a thick nerve that runs through the bones in the back

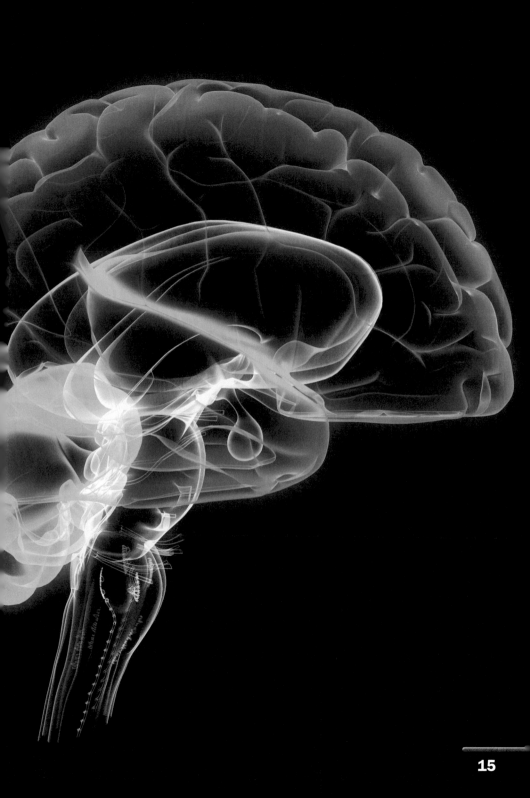

The reproductive system regulates the processes of the body that create new life. Each human being begins as two single cells—a cell from the mother and another cell from the father. When these two cells meet and combine, the gender of the baby is decided. Then, over a period of nine months, the cells grow larger, divide, and multiply to form various organs, muscles, and tissues. They continue to grow and develop until eventually a whole new entity is born: a baby.

During this period of cell development, strands of **DNA**[10] from the original two cells from the mother and father act like a set of **blueprints**,[11] telling the new cells what to do. DNA establishes the color of the baby's eyes, whether its hair is curly or straight—even the size of its smile. The result of this genetic mixing is a reproductive process that makes each human being a unique individual with his or her own individual physical and mental characteristics.

---

[10] **DNA:** *(Deoxyribonucleic acid),* the part of a cell that contains the genetic instructions used in the development and functioning of all known living organisms

[11] **blueprint:** a detailed drawing of something to show how to make it; a pattern

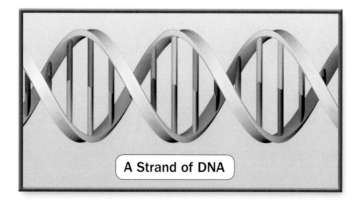

A Strand of DNA

Sequence the Events

What is the correct order of the events? Write numbers.

_____ A unique individual is born.

_____ The gender of the baby is decided.

_____ A cell from the mother and a cell from the father combine.

_____ The cells grow larger, divide, and multiply.

The organ systems of the body are complicated in their own right, but it's important to keep in mind that they don't only exist as individual units—they must all work together effectively. The final product of these coordinating systems is one unit that functions as a whole—the human body. Each of these systems depends on the others, either directly or indirectly, to keep the body functioning normally and healthily. It's all about efficiency, and it's all about coordination.

The end result of all of these corresponding systems and processes is a human body that is able to take us on an extraordinary journey every day. It allows us to push frontiers—both physical and mental—by doing things that we've never done before in new and exciting ways. It lets us meet remarkable challenges, and gives us the power to expand the limits of human achievement. And it all starts at the level of the single, little, cell.

After You Read

1. On page 4, swimming is given as an example of:
   A. the complex way in which the brain functions
   B. why it is so great to be a human
   C. the impressive way the body can move
   D. an action that only humans can do

2. In paragraph 1 on page 6, the word 'composed' means:
   A. operated
   B. made up
   C. adopted
   D. exploited

3. Which part of the body is NOT mentioned on page 6?
   A. heart
   B. bone
   C. tissue
   D. stomach

4. In paragraph 2, on page 9, 'our' in the phrase 'our lives' refers to:
   A. human beings
   B. heart pumps
   C. only writers
   D. only readers

5. The lungs deliver oxygen to the body _____ air passages.
   A. in
   B. by
   C. over
   D. through

6. Which of the following is the first step of the digestion process?
   A. Food is broken down into nutrients.
   B. Molecules get absorbed into the bloodstream.
   C. Food is converted into molecules.
   D. A bite of food is taken.

7. In paragraph 2 on page 14, 'they' is referring to:
   A. people
   B. brains
   C. automatic actions
   D. complex mental activities

8. Why does the writer point out that the brain looks like old fruit?
   A. to use humor to introduce a new topic
   B. to contrast its strange appearance with its great power
   C. to highlight a negative aspect of the brain
   D. to describe the exact size and shape of the brain

9. The word 'divide' in paragraph 1 on page 16 can be replaced by:
   A. expand
   B. coincide
   C. split
   D. append

10. Which of the following causes each individual born to be unique?
    A. genetic mixing
    B. cells
    C. mental characteristics
    D. fathers

11. What is the main purpose of paragraph 1 on page 19?
    A. to illustrate how the blood flows through the body
    B. to review how each organ's system works
    C. to explain how the body's parts rely on each other
    D. to discuss which organ is the most efficient

12. Which statement best summarizes the last sentence of the reader?
    A. The body is better than a machine.
    B. Humans are nothing more than a single cell.
    C. Great possibilities exist for the future of humans.
    D. A complex being has evolved from something simple and tiny.

Ask Dr. Jeffers

This month Dr. Jeffers is answering questions about the human brain and how it works.

DEAR DR. JEFFERS,

Someone told me that scientists are learning to use computers to 'read minds.' Is there any truth to this story?
–Jane Leon, New York, USA

DEAR MS. LEON,

Well, a lot of research is being conducted in this area, but so far, the brain scanning equipment and corresponding computer programs haven't been able to actually read thoughts. That said, researchers have made some impressive progress. In one experiment, test subjects were connected to scanning equipment and shown two numbers on a screen. They were then asked to choose between adding or subtracting the two numbers. Using this procedure, researchers were able to monitor brain processes and make the correct assumptions 70 percent of the time. It's not quite mind reading, but it's certainly a first step.
–Dr. J.

DEAR DR. JEFFERS,

My three-year-old son loves it when I dig my fingers into his sides and tickle him until he laughs uncontrollably. The other day I noticed him trying to tickle himself but he couldn't do it. Why not?
–Glenn Lewis,
  Vancouver, Canada

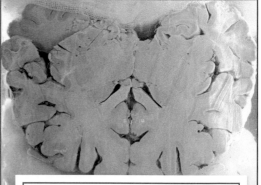

The left and right sides of a human brain look the same, but function differently.

Amazing Brain Facts	
1300-1400 g.	the average weight of a human brain
20%	the percentage of all the blood in the body needed for just the brain
100 billion +	the number of nerve cells in a human brain
18	the age at which the brain stops growing
25%	the percentage of the brain used to control the eyes alone

DEAR MR. LEWIS,

It's because of how the brain works. The brain is trained to know what to pay attention to and what to ignore. It causes us to ignore physical feelings we expect to happen, but it causes a mild panic reaction when there is an unexpected feeling. For example, you don't notice how your shoulder feels while you're walking down the street. But if someone comes up behind you and taps you lightly on the shoulder, you may jump in fright. It's that unexpected part that also causes the tickle reaction.

–Dr. J.

DEAR DR. JEFFERS,

I have heard that some people are 'right brain' people and others are 'left brain' people. What do these terms mean?

–Felix Moeller, Essen, Germany

DEAR MR. MOELLER,

Scientists have studied the two halves of the brain and determined that the left side is mostly concerned with logical, rational, and analytical tasks. On the other hand, the right side of the brain seems to function in a more random and subjective mode, and is mostly responsible for emotions and imagination. Although some people seem to find one style of thinking more natural, research shows that we all use both sides of the brain in all of the mental tasks we perform.

–Dr. J.

CD 3, Track 04

Word Count: 406
Time: _____

Vocabulary List

acid (13, 16)
bloodstream (9, 13)
blueprint (16)
cell (2, 6, 9, 10, 13, 14, 16, 17, 19)
circulatory system (3, 6, 9)
digestive system (3, 6, 10, 13, 14)
DNA (16)
enzyme (13)
epithelial (6)
lungs (2, 4, 6, 9)
molecule (10, 12, 13)
muscle (2, 4, 6, 9, 16)
nervous system (3, 6, 14)
nourishment (10, 12, 13)
nutrient (10, 12, 13)
organ (2, 3, 6, 9, 10, 16, 19)
reproductive system (3, 6, 16)
respiratory system (3, 6, 9)
spinal cord (14)
swallow (13)
tissue (2, 6, 16)
trillion (2, 6)

Metric Conversion Chart

Area
1 hectare = 2.471 acres

Length
1 centimeter = .394 inches
1 meter = 1.094 yards
1 kilometer = .621 miles

Temperature
0° Celsius = 32° Fahrenheit

Volume
1 liter = 1.057 quarts

Weight
1 gram = .035 ounces
1 kilogram = 2.2 pounds